Praise for *Dear Ole Miss*

Sam's storytelling style is unique. It's like you are sitting across the kitchen table as he tells you his latest adventure. And what adventures: on the football field, in the classroom, making plans for life after college. —W.J. Humphrey, author of the *Wright Family Saga* series

I've known you a long time. Man, did we have fun together. Dear Ole Miss *triggered many of those fabulous memories. All good ones and you're still going strong. —*Val S. Cuthbert, Oxford, Mississippi

I thoroughly enjoyed reading Dear Ole Miss. You are a born storyteller and now I know you're a gifted author. Those stories are so heartwarming. —Neal Sumner, Oxford, Mississippi

Thank you for writing Dear Ole Miss. My first thought was about when we met because you married my roommate, Judy. I loved your stories. —Hicky Wallace, Delta Gamma, Ole Miss Cheerleader, Oxford, Mississippi

*You're still telling great stories, but now they're in book form. I love them. Keep on keeping on boy. —*Josh Bogan, Oxford, Mississippi

*In this personal history of Ole Miss in the early 1960s, Sam Owen captures with humor and awe the glory of campus life just as he lived it. Sam's stories brought back fond memories of my own college days (even though I attended another SEC school). —*Sandra Whitten Plant, author of *Sweet Adversity: A Southern Writer Finds Stories–and Good–in Everything*

Praise for *Old Times Not Forgotten*

What a memory jog into the fun-filled days of my own innocent Southern childhood. Each story is simply uplifting and good for one's soul . . . A "Song of the South." —Donna Kirkland Cantrell

People from Mississippi like to tell stories. Sam and I grew up in the same hometown. That being said, I can attest to the fact that the stories in this book are absolutely the truth. They are delightful, and so is Sam! —Sarah Wilkinson

Sam's stories…have brought laughter and a few tears. His Mississippi heritage is a rich source of vibrant stories. —Lucy Majors, co-author of *Baby Boy Majors*

A wonderful collection of small-town Mississippi tales that will entertain anyone curious about the deep South and its culture. Sam finds humor and irony in so many everyday experiences he has loved and embedded in his memory. He's a genuine "Mississippi boy" willing to share an appreciation of his eventful life and journey through it. —Beverly McKenzie

Sam is a born storyteller. From his early years growing up in Mississippi, his high school adventures in Oak Ridge, Tennessee, and his experiences as a football hero at Ole Miss, Sam has collected a lifetime of engaging stories. They are laced with Sam's natural humor and embedded with his profound wisdom and ethical values, which propelled his success as a healthcare executive. This book is entertainment at its best! You are guaranteed to enjoy getting to know Sam as much as I have! —Lisa Atkinson

Sam has experienced a life that many of us would envy—from growing up in Mississippi, to hopping a freight train, to taking down a bully and so much more. His stories capture the joy he's experienced in a life well lived. —W.J. Humphrey, author of the *Wright Family Saga* series

Dear Ole Miss

Dear Ole Miss

Samuel Walton Owen

Knoxville, Tennessee, USA
crippledbeaglepublishing.com

Cover artwork by Roger Ryskamp
About the cover artwork: The Lyceum building, completed in 1848, is the oldest building on the Ole Miss campus. Students from the university's founding in 1848 to the present revere this Greek Revival structure as a historic and beloved symbol. First used as a classroom building, the Lyceum now houses the university's administrative offices.

Paperback ISBN 978-1-965334-27-0, 978-1-965334-28-7
Hardcover ISBN 978-1-965334-29-4, 978-1-965334-30-0
ePub ISBN 978-1-965334-36-2

Library of Congress Control Number: 2025900735

Printed in the United States of America

Stories

Thank you to my late parents, Walton and Corinne Owen. Without their love and support this book would not have been possible.

Thank you to my wife, Judy, the love of my life for more than sixty years, for encouraging me to write these stories.

To my family, these stories are for you. I love y'all

Sam's parents Walton and Corinne Owen sit on the steps of their home in Norris, Tennessee. On Mama Corinne's lap is her pet chihuahua, Speedy Gonzales.

The procession of the Ole Miss Rebels football team through the Walk of Champions in The Grove at Ole Miss on their way to the stadium is a highlight for tailgaters on Game Day. Sam and Judy Owen had the idea for this campus landmark and provided funding for its construction.

We are Rebels through and through,

Even our blood runs Red and Blue.

There's nothing finer in this land,

Than loyal and gracious Ole Miss fans.

—Samuel Walton Owen

The Owen family tailgates in The Grove before an Ole Miss football game. From left to right: son Jeff, Judy, son Bryan, Sam, and son Parkes. Both Parkes and Bryan are Ole Miss grads. Jeff graduated from SEC school, Vanderbilt University, in Nashville, Tennessee.

Dear Ole Miss,

This is a love letter from a family that cherishes our beloved alma mater. You have been an integral part of our lives. First, I want to thank you for giving me the education, life lessons, and friendships that have propelled me to a successful career and a happy life. Next, thank you for being the magical place where I met, fell in love with, and married the fabulous Judy Josephson. You've been a major part of our lives for almost sixty-five years

You brought Judy and me together as sweethearts in 1960, our sophomore year. We became husband and wife three years later. You have wrapped your arms around two of our children, two daughters by marriage, two of our granddaughters, and other relatives who are now your alumni and friends. What a legacy we share!

My sister, Rosemary "Rusty" Owen, was an Ole Miss Favorite and feature twirler with the Pride of the South Band. Our sons, Bryan and Parkes, were members of the same fraternity. Bryan was captain and kicker for the Rebel football team. Our sons met our wonderful daughters-in-law at Ole Miss; Bryan married Britton Ousley and Parkes wed Rebecca Portis.

Two of our granddaughters received their diplomas in the historic Grove, as we all did. Bryan and Britton's daughters, Anniston "Annie" Owen and Mary Ousley "Momo" Owen, love you just as much as their parents and grandparents do.

Another important connection you'll read about later is my mother, Corinne Parkes Owen, who served as Pi Kappa Alpha housemother for fifteen happy years. Don't be surprised if a few more Owens come your way in the future.

You never speak out loud; you just let your warm hospitality and beautiful campus do your talking for you. Our Ole Miss is special to all of us. Your warmth and beauty need to be celebrated; that's why I wrote this book of stories—so you will know that wherever we may be, our hearts are with you.

Love,
Sam Owen

Sam Sees His Future

I was just a little kid the first time Daddy took me to an Ole Miss football game. That's the day I saw a big banner hanging at the entrance to the campus. I've never forgotten those words: "Welcome to Ole Miss, where everybody speaks!"

I asked my daddy what that sign meant. He thought for a minute. "Doc, those words are the difference maker between Ole Miss and other schools."

Just as soon as Daddy and I started walking to Hemingway Stadium, I understood. Folks in our hometown of New Albany were friendly, but nothing like the people we met on the Ole Miss campus. Everyone had a spring in their step. They were smiling and happy. Everyone spoke.

I knew then that I wanted more than anything to be on that welcoming campus, to play football at Hemingway Stadium, to walk to classes on that beautiful campus, to go to parties and dances. I wanted to be in that happy place.

Fast forward to 1959 when I was enrolled as a student (a student with a coveted football scholarship). As my parents and I arrived on campus and headed toward my new home at Miller Hall, I saw that sign. "Welcome to Ole Miss, where everybody speaks!" I had made it to my happy place.

On his first visit to Ole Miss at age seven, young Sam sits on the lap of Sue Parkes, his cousin's pretty wife.

Daddy Speaks, Sam Listens

One day, Daddy came to me for one of his many chats about things to do with my life. Although he was quite interested in all my activities, he rarely dictated what I should or shouldn't do. He left those decisions to me, because he had faith in me. That was one of the greatest qualities about my daddy; he trusted me as I did him.

But this day was two days before the start of fall football practice for the 1957 season. It was my junior year of high school. Daddy said, "Doc, you and I need to have a talk. Get in the truck. We're going for a ride to talk about your future."

After a lengthy ride, a long chat, and a lot of thought and consternation, I said, "Yes sir, I think that makes a lot of sense. I'll go talk to Coach Armstrong tomorrow about me playing football."

My high school football career began two days later. After my first practice, I was convinced that I had made the worst mistake of my life. I thought I was going to die. But Daddy's golden rule was now in effect: "You can't quit what you start."

Thank goodness I stuck it out. Listening to Daddy on that day made a huge difference in my life.

Sam Signs with Ole Miss

My goal in life was to be an Ole Miss Rebel football player. I wanted to wear the best-looking football uniform ever made. I wanted to play in Tiger Stadium in Baton Rouge and beat LSU. I wanted to play at Shields-Watkins Field in Knoxville and beat Tennessee before a sell-out crowd of 55,000 people in Neyland Stadium.

I wanted to play in the Sugar Bowl in New Orleans, and I wanted to win it. I wanted to win the SEC championship, and the national championship. I also wanted to win the Tennessee state football championship and the high school national championship. Those were my dreams in life, and guess what? Every single one of them came true.

Now, let me set the stage for how this phenomenal period of my life began. It started at midnight on December 6, 1958, the National Signing Day set by the NCAA for all colleges and universities to grant football scholarships to prospective players. It was a hectic time, because of the incredible competition for the signatures of the top players around the country, and those of their parents or guardians.

I signed my Ole Miss scholarship that night along with two of my high school teammates, Lewis Lanter and Skippy Brinkman. We were sitting in the living room of Ole Miss alumnus O.V. Young and in the company of coaches who represented a number of top football universities: Tennessee, Alabama, Florida State, North Carolina, and Georgia Tech, as well as Ole Miss. All of them were trying to convince us to sign with their respective school.

When the clock struck midnight, Coach Johnny "Hurry" Cain of Ole Miss stood up and put a scholarship and an Ole Miss pen in front of Lewis, Skippy, and me. "There's your ticket to the best place in the world," he said. "Sign it, or regret it the rest of your life. I have other people to sign tonight. Y'all can be first."

My decision had never been in doubt. We all signed with Ole Miss. Coach Cain also signed our classmate Nancy Anne Reed to a full majorette scholarship to perform for the Ole Miss Rebel Band.

Signing with Ole Miss was the most exciting and rewarding event in my life. It was also an exciting event for my mama and daddy. My daddy, Walton, had always wanted to play football for Ole Miss, but he was too small; so, as he put it, "I'll now get to play for the Rebels through Sam."

Ole Miss Welcomes the Owen Siblings, 1948 and 1959

Almost one hundred years to the day after the first eighty students enrolled at the University of Mississippi in 1848, my older sister Rosemary began her freshman year at Ole Miss.

It was a beautiful fall day in 1948 when my parents, Rosemary, and I left our home in New Albany, just thirty miles east of Oxford. Driving on the gravel road that linked the two towns, Daddy led the caravan of three cars on this glorious morning.

Everyone was excited. Rosemary was beside herself, and Mama and Daddy had mixed emotions. Our household helpers, Vergie and Roscoe, rode behind in a panel truck hauling my sister's clothes. I had never seen so much girlie stuff in my life. I sure didn't have that much boy stuff, and I didn't want it.

I was only seven years old at the time. I remember vividly my first look at the Ole Miss campus; it was the prettiest place I'd ever seen in my life. The beauty of the place cinched it for me. I decided right then that I was going to attend Ole Miss someday and play football for the Ole Miss Rebels.

Living her own dream, Rosemary made her mark on Ole Miss. As the band's featured twirler, she drove football fans wild on game day when my gorgeous sister strutted onto the field, copper-colored hair blazing, her smile flashing like a lighthouse beacon.

Eleven years later, I arrived on campus with my parents and my friend and football teammate, Skippy Brinkman. It was then that I knew how Rosemary felt on that beautiful fall day in 1948 when she arrived on this heavenly campus.

The Dean of Freshmen, a Legend at Ole Miss

Ole Miss has many traditions, but a favorite of my boyhood was paying our respects to the Dean of Freshmen. This was not a position officially associated with the University: "Dean of Freshmen" was the self-bestowed title of James "Blind Jim" Ivy, a black peanut vendor who was cherished by loyal alumni, visiting fans, and students. It was customary for all to pay their respect to Blind Jim and receive the Dean's permission to come on campus. Jim died in 1955, but he was a fixture on campus for more than fifty years.

Jim was blinded in an accident when he was around thirteen years old; but after all his years cheering for Ole Miss, he joked, "I ain't never seen the Rebels lose a game."

Old photos of Jim show a distinguished gentleman dressed like a Southern planter, wearing a gray suit with matching vest and a wide-brimmed hat. His dark complexion was set off by a full white mustache, a trademark of our beloved Dean of Freshmen.

For every game, against every opponent, Jim would always create a cheer or greeting appropriate to the occasion. If we were playing Arkansas, the cheer was, "Whole hog, half a ham. Arkansas ain't wuf a damn." If Alabama was the enemy Jim would say, "Yellahammer, Yellahammer, to hell with Alabammer." (The yellowhammer is the state bird of Alabama.)

Whenever my parents and I headed to Ole Miss to see the Rebels play, Daddy would be almost as excited as I was. We had a ritual that we followed for each game we attended. We arrived in The Grove early the morning of the game. Cars were allowed to park in The Grove back then; Mama and Daddy would select a perfect spot and set up the tailgate on card tables we had brought with us.

My friends and I would pass a football while waiting on the feast of fried chicken, potato salad, pimiento cheese sandwiches, and Mama's fabulous stuffed boiled eggs. There were plenty of beverages for everyone; but some were made with brown water, clear water, and ice.

Once our bellies were full, the next ritual was getting Jim's permission to enter the campus. As I recall, Jim could recognize his many friends by just hearing their voices. I remember him recognizing my daddy every time we saw him. One day Daddy turned the tables on Jim. He asked him, "You still messing around that woman with a wooden leg?"

"What you talking about?"

Daddy said, "That's why you got all those splinters in your hand."

They both fell out laughing. Jim never said where the splinters came from because there weren't any. He let it dangle so they could both enjoy the joke again at the next game.

High Cotton and a Victory

Our chartered planes landed at Lexington, Kentucky's airport on a beautiful Friday afternoon. It was September 29, 1961.

The airport was near Calumet Farms, the home of some of horse racing's most famous thoroughbreds. None of us had ever seen farms so beautiful. Now we knew what a Kentucky horse farm looked like. with its lush bluegrass, beautiful white barns, and white, wooden fences. A far cry from a Mississippi Delta cotton plantation, but both were pretty in their own ways.

But we weren't there to see horse farms. We were in Lexington to put some whoop-ass on the Kentucky Wildcats.

The buses took us directly to the University of Kentucky's field house, so we could change into our workout uniforms. We were shocked at the small size and stifling heat of the visitors' locker room. It was embarrassing to us; but it drove home which sport was at the top of the heap in Lexington: Coach Adolph Rupp's basketball team. Football was an afterthought.

After changing clothes, we went to the gym before working out in the stadium. At least the gym was cooler.

We noticed a familiar-looking man and a young blonde guy working on jump shots. The guy never missed. All we heard was the swish of the net.

The older man came over to talk with me and two of my teammates, since we were closest to him. It was Coach Rupp himself. He was a nice fellow. He wanted to chat with us about the game the next night.

We asked him who the player was shooting jump shots. He answered with a big grin. "He's one of my freshman signees. I'm teaching him how to refine his jump shot. You'll know who he is next year, when he can play varsity ball for us. Remember his name, because he's special. His name is Cotton Nash."

Coach Adolph Rupp went on to say, "He'll be a star like the quarterbacks on your football team."

Coach Rupp turned to return to practice. "Good luck tomorrow night. You've got a great team, but we may beat you.

We laughed and said, "We'll see."

Final score: Ole Miss 20, UK 6.

Notes

Cotton Nash was the University of Kentucky's leading scorer when his career there ended (a record he owned for the next six years). He was named All-American in all three seasons he played for the Wildcats.

Adolph Rupp became a legendary coach during his forty-one-year coaching career. He was named to the Basketball Hall of Fame in 1969 and the College Basketball Hall of Fame in 2006.

High School Stars Fall to Earth

The varsity football players laid out the welcome mat for us freshmen. They set up a barber shop for us to receive our new haircuts. It was outfitted with clippers and several chairs.

The Freshmen Welcoming Party began with the disappearance of ducktails and side parts once the clippers were turned on. The new hairstyles were funny, especially the bald heads on the cocky ones with one ducktail remaining.

Then they brought out the big wooden paddles with "Ole Miss" engraved deep in the wood. We soon learned there was nothing funny about those paddles. One of the requirements for each of us was to balance a glass of water filled to the brim in the small of our backs while grabbing our ankles. Then the varsity assholes struck several blows to each freshman's naked butt. If the water spilled, they added a lick. Thank God, I didn't spill any water. To this day, I don't know how I managed it, but I'm glad I did.

We were all hurting and humiliated after the paddling. That's the reason eleven freshmen sneaked out of Miller Hall that first night and never returned. I also had my doubts about staying at Ole Miss. Hazing sucked. Remarkably, none of us had known anything about it while we were being recruited.

I considered leaving, but decided I wasn't quitting; nobody could make me do that except head coach Johnny Vaught. I was determined to live out my lifelong dream, and no one was going to deprive me of that. I just prayed every night that I could endure the hazing.

That night I swore to the Big Guy above that I would never haze anyone as long as I lived. Consequently, hazing started to die out during my sophomore year at Ole Miss. I paddled one freshman that first night, but after that, I didn't haze any freshmen assigned to me throughout my time at Ole Miss. I set a new standard, and I'm proud of that.

That's when I realized that I was a leader, because others followed suit. The paddling began to disappear. Although the freshmen football players still had to carry out their valet jobs and do other things the varsity players demanded, paddling wasn't a part of their worries—unless they got cocky. Woe be unto them if that happened.

The First Time Ever I Saw Your Face

On Wednesday, September 16, 1959, the Sigma Alpha Epsilon fraternity had a swap with our sister sorority, Delta Gamma. Normally, football practice ran late, so I hadn't planned to attend the swap. We didn't have time for social activity; all freshmen football players were required to attend study hall and be in our rooms by 9:30 every night with lights out at 10 p.m..

But for some reason, study hall was canceled on this day, and I didn't have any homework, a rare occurrence, to say the least. I had a free night until 9:30.

I didn't know what to do with my free time, because football practice had also ended early. Consequently, being the party animal that I am, I decided to go to the swap.

As I entered the SAE house with some of my teammates, the music was blaring and the party was well underway. We wouldn't be able to tarry very long because we had to be back in Miller Hall for bed check.

As we made our way into the SAE house to engage in the festive evening and mingle with everyone, our SAE brothers offered us Busch Bavarian beer. Although we all wanted a beer, none of us accepted their hospitality; if Coach Wobble Davidson smelled beer on our breath at bed check, it would be the ultimate lights-out and the end of our Ole Miss football careers.

After some fun chit-chat with my SAE pledge brothers, I decided to saunter over toward the dance floor, which was in the large sunken living room of the house. I wanted to watch the girls dancing to the music coming over the new sound system. The song was "Big Boss Man" by Jimmy Reed; it had a fantastic beat, written perfectly for those of us who loved to dance the shag, the coolest dance step ever known to man.

As I stood there looking over the dance floor, it happened; from out of nowhere, I saw the cutest girl that I had ever seen in my life. Cupid's arrow found its target, piercing my heart. Miraculously, it hasn't moved one iota since then; it's still in place, doing its job.

I was frozen in my tracks. I felt like Gomer Pyle saying, "Shazam! Shazam! Shazam!"

I turned to one of my pledge brother teammates and asked, "Who is that little blonde girl dancing with Fred Towle?"

His reply was instantaneous. "Her name is Judy Josephson." He then told me, "She's a Yankee from Chicargo." That's the Mississippi pronunciation of "Chicago."

"Are you sure about that?" I asked. "I thought all girls from Chicargo were big and ugly, and that's the exact opposite of what I'm seeing."

Whether or not my friend was correct about the girl's identity and origin, she sure as hell wasn't ugly. Judy

33

Josephson was adorable. She was dainty, petite, and beautiful, with Swedish ancestry. Her complexion was a stunning tan, similar to the color of a hazelnut and smooth as cream. Those features were accentuated by her feisty natural blonde hair. Her angelic face radiated her beauty, her happiness, and her kindness. She was about five feet tall, with a well-proportioned figure. In other words, she was a knockout.

I fell in love with her the moment I saw her. Too bad my head was shaved and I looked like a rat; I was too embarrassed about the way I looked to introduce myself, thanks to the hazing of the freshmen football players.

Because of those circumstances, I didn't take the opportunity to meet her. Besides, I had to leave the party; it was almost 9:30. There was no way in hell I was going to lose my scholarship because I was at a frat party chasing a girl I didn't even know.

I left the SAE party with my teammates; we only had fifteen minutes before the doors of Miller Hall would be locked. We ran as fast as we could to get back. Thank God, we made it just in the nick of time.

Coach "Wobble" Davidson arrived at the entry door at the same time we did. He had his key in hand just as I burst into the hallway. Coach Wobble was his typical, jovial self: "You sons-of-bitches almost got your Greyhound Bus tickets home. Get your asses in your rooms. Now!" he hollered. "Chasing girls will get you in a lot of trouble around here. Then you'll be gone."

Coach Wobble did his job well because he loved it. He scared the living hell out of all of us that night with his warm, fatherly advice. He kept every Ole Miss football player, freshman and varsity alike, in line with just the right amount of fear.

It was like that for the rest of the time we were at Ole Miss. To this day, I believe Coach Wobble's management of Miller Hall was one of the major factors in Ole Miss's longstanding prominence and success on the national football scene.

I didn't see Judy Josephson again during the remainder of my freshman year. Unfortunately, being a freshman football player at Ole Miss wasn't easy. It damn sure wasn't any fun. It consumed every minute of my life for the entire year.

Sam and Judy Get Together at Last

The varsity football players had welcomed us freshmen football signees in 1959 by shaving our heads and eyebrows and beating us brutally with paddles made just for such occasions. Normally, I was an outgoing, happy person, but I didn't want to meet anyone, especially girls, when I looked like something from your worst nightmare.

Now that my freshman year was behind me, I returned to Ole Miss in August of 1960 for my sophomore year with renewed courage. My new hair and eyebrows tagged along for the ride.

I finally got to meet and date that fabulous girl I had dreamed of since early in my freshman year when I dropped in on the swap at the SAE house with our sister sorority, the Delta Gammas.

I wasn't much to look at when I spotted that precious, petite, blonde on the dance floor the year before. But this was a new day, a new time, and a new year. That had to be a significant sign of something.

The DGs were a cool bunch of adorable girls. They seemed to always come up with fun and festive parties with the SAEs and the football team.

This year's party for the football team was held in spring, when the Ole Miss campus was gloriously beautiful. The music was fabulous, and that added lots of excitement in the air.

Because we were guests in their sorority house, it was expected that the DGs would ask us guys to dance, and even cut in if they desired. I was dancing with one of my good friends when someone tapped her on the shoulder to cut in on me.

Holy cow! It was her. That cute thing I had seen last year, when I looked like Igor. She must have noticed something that appealed to her, because she said, "Hi! I'm Judy Josephson. What's your name?"

I told her my name, but it wasn't easy to say anything else, because she had swept me off my feet. She was so cute. Her eyes were blue and sparkly. Her smile reminded me of a string of pearls. I didn't know what she saw in me; but there must have been something, or we wouldn't be where we were at this moment.

After a couple of dances Judy suggested that we adjourn to the swing on the front porch where we could talk. The evening air was balmy. It worked; we were both happy, and I was smitten. I thought to myself, I just fell in love with a girl from Flossmoor, Illinois. A Yankee. What was I going to tell my daddy?

I didn't care. This girl wasn't getting away from me. After the evening at the DG house came to an end, I had to hurry to Miller Hall for bed check and to make a quick phone call.

The phone rang three times, and I recognized her voice. I said, "Good night, Judy. I sure did have fun tonight."

"Me too. Good night!"

I stood there holding the receiver in my hand, staring at nothing.

Coach Wobble snapped me back to reality: "Hang up the damn phone and get your ass to your room."

"Yes sir, Coach. Good night. Judy said to tell you hi."

Coach Wobble didn't laugh. "Meet me at the stadium tomorrow at half past three," he said. "You're running twenty laps for missing bed check."

It was worth it. I met the girl of my dreams and learned that One + One = One. We were married on June 1, 1963.

Meet Mr. Soupbone and Ms. Bullet

Ole Miss has many traditions; my favorite is nicknames. Almost everybody I knew during my time at Ole Miss was given a nickname, especially those of us on the football team.

My college nickname at Ole Miss was Soupbone. Here's how it happened. When my class of freshman football players arrived on campus in1959, the first official gathering that night was the varsity players' Freshmen Welcome Party. That's when we got our new haircuts and our "welcome to Ole Miss" paddling,

When my name was called to get my haircut, I took my seat and waited for the buzzing sound to start. In less than thirty seconds my entire head was shaved to the skin or worse. It hurt like hell. It was thorough. It was quick. Everybody started cackling, hollering, and howling with laughter.

I didn't know why until Reggie Robertson, a varsity running back, jumped up and yelled, "Hey y'all! Look at that freshman's head. It looks just like the end of a damn soupbone."

Then he followed up with, "Hey freshman, from now on you're gonna be called Soupbone. If you don't like that, we can adjust your attitude for you."

I yelled back at him, "I love my new nickname!"

That did it. I've been Soupbone ever since. My nickname is now sixty-four years old and still going strong. I'm sure that Saint Peter will welcome me at the pearly gates with, "Look who just arrived y'all. It's Soupbone!"

I've stated many times how adorable Judy is. She's so petite—just five feet tall, by her account. One day Reggie came up to me in front of the Grill and asked me, "Hey, Soupbone, who's that cute little blonde thing you're going with?"

I told him Judy's name. Then Reggie said to me, "Damn, son. She's the cutest thing I've seen in a long time. She reminds me of a twenty-two short rifle bullet. You know what? She's gettin' a nickname. From now on that cute thing is gonna have a nickname to go along with yours. We're gonna call her Bullet!"

It stuck. To this day, Judy and I are known to our many friends who knew us at Ole Miss as Soupbone and Bullet!

A Picnic with Coach Wobble

In 1959, my freshman year at Ole Miss, I lived in Miller Hall, the athletic dorm. One of the simplest but most important rules at Miller Hall was that there was no eating allowed in dorm rooms. Period! No exceptions! No excuses!

The punishment for the first offense was twenty laps in twenty minutes, up and down the sixty-four rows of seats in Hemingway Stadium, with the perpetrator dressed in full uniform, with shoulder pads, helmet, and cleats. You started at row one and had to run the steps to the top and back down to complete a single lap. Twenty laps. That was beyond brutal!

The person doing the supervising and timing was the legendary coach J. W. "Wobble" Davidson.

Our opportunity to run those laps began when my roommate, Skippy Brinkman, and I were reminiscing about favorite meals. We both loved peanut-butter-and-banana sandwiches with mayonnaise.

Nothing tasted better to us than one of those sandwiches chased down with a great big glass of ice-cold milk. We began plotting to get ourselves some peanut-butter-and-banana sandwiches and milk that night after Coach Wobble had completed rounds for bed check and turned in for the night.

I assumed responsibility for procuring the necessary supplies for our feast. I got a friend to take me to City Grocery Store on the Square; then I went back to Miller Hall and sneaked the supplies into the dorm. Skippy and I concluded that the outside temperature was cool enough to serve as a refrigerator until feast time. We put the stuff out on the window ledge of our second-floor room.

On cue, at 9:30 p.m., Coach Wobble came by our room to make his final bed check, then left to return to his apartment. We waited until 10 p.m. to make our move. We fixed our room so the lights couldn't be seen, draping blankets over the space between our twin beds. We kept one small gooseneck lamp directed so we could see to prepare our feast without being noticed.

Soon, our banquet was ready. I did a masterful job with the sandwiches. Skippy and I both took big bites of fresh bread encasing those sweet bananas, the gooey peanut butter, and the delicious mayonnaise, chasing it with the cold milk. Oh my gosh! What a treat!

Skippy mumbled through his gooey mouthful, "Is this the best thing we've eaten in months?"

Before we could take another bite, we heard a weird, eerie sound. "What's that?" I asked, startled.

Talk about an "Oh, shit" moment! The blanket draped over the space between our twin beds began to move. Suddenly, it was yanked away; our little lamp shone on a figure towering six feet, three inches above us. It was Coach Wobble. The strange noise we had heard was his master key opening the lock to our room. Our goose (not the gooseneck lamp), our peanut-butter-and-banana sandwiches, and our asses were cooked.

Coach Wobble just stood there glaring at us. Then he asked in a very calm voice, "What are you two doing?" We couldn't speak for two reasons. One was fear. The other was because our mouths were full of peanut butter, bananas, and bread with mayonnaise. Feebly I answered, "Eating peanut-butter-and-banana sandwiches."

Uncharacteristically, Coach Wobble said in a very calm, rational voice, "I'll see y'all at the stadium tomorrow at three-thirty, in full uniform. Now, turn out your lights and go to bed." He disappeared quietly. "Good night. See you tomorrow."

We were shocked. He didn't appear to be angry at all. What was going on?

The next day, Skippy and I looked like we were ready to play a football game. The managers outfitted us in game uniforms: blue jerseys with white numerals and white shoulder stripes. The Ole Miss grey pants with red and blue stripes on the sides looked really cool. We arrived on time, at 3:30 p.m.

Coach Wobble was waiting for us in the stadium. He told us to have a seat as he explained the reasons for the rules. Then he blew his whistle, and we started running up, then down, the stadium steps. After four laps Coach Wobble did something quite unusual. He told us to sit down and take a breather for a minute or two. We happily did as we were told.

After a couple of minutes, Coach got up and walked over to a place about twenty feet away. He reached underneath the stadium seats and retrieved two brown paper grocery sacks. He handed each of us a sack and told us to open it.

Coach Wobble said, "I just gave you bastards twenty fucking peanut-butter-and-banana sandwiches with lots of mayonnaise on 'em. You also got a quart of milk. Now start running. Eat a sandwich on every lap and chase it with milk. Then let's see how much you like eating that shit in your room. Start running, start eating, and start drinking that milk!"

I don't know how we did it, but somehow, we finished our assignment. We threw up a bunch of times, which helped. I couldn't eat another peanut-butter-and-banana sandwich for years after that ordeal.

Thank goodness, years later I overcame my aversion. PB&B sandwiches are now back on my favorites list. I suppose it's a Mississippi thing. Elvis loved 'em, too.

Daddy Sets Me Straight

Unfortunately, being a freshman football player at Ole Miss wasn't easy. It consumed every minute of my life during my freshman year. During that first year, I seriously considered leaving Ole Miss on numerous occasions, but my daddy always squelched those yearnings after we talked it through.

This time was different. Football sucked, hazing sucked, and my life sucked because I was tired of getting whacked with a paddle by some varsity asshole every night. I swore to myself that someday I would get even; but after further thought, I decided I would just quit football and go home. I was done. I was finished. Kaput. I went to a payphone and called home (collect) to break the news to my folks that I was quitting.

It was so reassuring to hear Mama's sweet, calming voice telling the operator that she would accept the collect call from her little darling. Following the sweet greeting from my mama, I told her that I was quitting football and coming home. I'm not sure what I expected her to say: maybe Oh Sam, that's wonderful news. Come on home. But instead, she said, "Here's your Daddy. You tell him that."

Oops! This would require a quick change of approach. Should I zig, zag, or just hang up?

My dad was glad to hear my voice, but he wondered why I was calling home. Was something wrong? I opened my canned speech with a well-practiced spiel. I told my dad that

I needed some money to get a plane ticket on Southern Airways to fly to Knoxville.

His "What for?" stumped me. Plane tickets weren't cheap, but my story was. I explained to him that I was leaving Ole Miss to come home.

My dad's answer was startling and unexpected to this naive freshman; but it was quite sobering. It was purely my daddy. He listened intently and patiently, two characteristics that weren't among his strong suits. He listened and interjected a well-placed "Uh-huh," or "I see," at the perfect place, at the perfect time during my spiel.

After I finished my story and paused for a long time, my dad asked me if I was through talking. "Yessir," I said.

He then said he had something to say to me about a scholarship. I was elated for that, because it appeared that my dad understood my plight. He then told me that he wasn't surprised at my decision to quit, because he never thought that I was tough enough to play college football anyway. He then told me that a quitter is a piece of shit.

I was startled. This wasn't going the way I had planned it. That's when he hit me with a left hook, uppercut to the jaw, and belt in my gut.

"You go get your quittin' ass on a Greyhound Bus to Knoxville and I'll be there waiting on you with a scholarship you can't quit," he said. "Your quitting ass will be getting on the next bus going to Parris Island, South Carolina, to a scholarship in the United States Marine Corps. I'd like to see you quit that scholarship." Then he slammed the phone down on me!

I needed to make a decision. My mom and dad were on the same sheet of music but not on the same page as me. Considering my choices—crawling and wading through the swampy marshes of Parris Island or playing the game of football on a manicured football field at Ole Miss—the conclusion was a no-brainer. The football field at Ole Miss won in a landslide.

I had just needed someone to explain the difference in simple language. That scholarship looked awfully nice once my dad 'splained it to me. I understood; I stayed. And I am so glad I did. Thank you, Daddy!

Butterflies from Hell

It was the first football game of the 1961 season for Ole Miss, and the Game of the Week on ABC national television. Bud Palmer was the broadcaster.

Ole Miss was playing Arkansas in Jackson, Mississippi. The temperature on the field was well over 100 degrees. It was my first football game as a redshirt sophomore. The butterflies in my stomach felt the size of bald eagles flapping their wings.

Coaches Bruiser Kinard and Buster Poole kept telling us, "You better be ready, 'cause you're gonna be in the game before you know it." But contrary to what the coaches had been telling us, none of us redshirt sophomores actually thought we would get to play.

Early in the second quarter, I heard Coach Vaught's distinctive voice yell, "Soupbone! Soupbone!"

My great friend, the center and inside linebacker Kenny Dill, hit me in the chest. "Hey Soup, Slick's calling yo name," he said. "Getcha ass up there, you dumbass. He's gonna put you in."

I didn't believe that, so I ambled up to Coach Vaught's side and asked, "Did you call my name, Coach?"

Coach Vaught turned to me, his mouth full of orders; but an astonished look spread across his face, and for a moment he was speechless. He then yelled, "You dumb sombitch!

You gonna play without a hat? Go get your damn helmet on!"

I felt a sudden wave of elation, excitement, nervousness, and focus engulf my body. I wheeled around and sprinted to the bench to get my helmet.

Suddenly, the feelings that had filled my heart, mind, and soul with emotion turned to nausea and fear.

Oh crap! What does this mean?

As I bent down to get my helmet it happened.

I vomited. Not on the bench, not on my shoes, not on the grass, but inside my beautiful powder-blue helmet with a red stripe down the middle. It was awful.

Despite what I had just deposited in my helmet, I didn't hesitate. I dumped it on the ground and put my helmet on, then raced back to Coach Vaught's side and said, "I'm ready, Coach. What do you want me to do?"

He almost threw up himself from the revolting smell as I came near. He was gagging as he gave me my instructions: "Cause a fumble."

I did. I recovered it. The referee shouted, "First down, Ole Miss!"

A Mystery Letter from Dothan, Alabama

Several days following our trouncing of Mississippi State, a.k.a., "Cow College," I went to the Student Union to check my mail. When I opened my mailbox, there was a nine-by-eleven white envelope covered in three-cent stamps. It was simply addressed by hand:

Sam Owen #60

Ole Miss Rebel

I couldn't believe the envelope found its way to me at Ole Miss with that meager address on it. There was no return address, but it was postmarked Dothan, Alabama. Wonder what's in it? Wonder who sent it?

When I tore open the envelope, I found a treasure inside. It was a picture of me intercepting my first pass in a college football game. The photo was a part of Hollis Curl's exciting article describing Ole Miss's big win over the Cow College Rednecks in 1962. The pass had been intended for Mississippi State's All-American end, Johnny Baker, who went on to stardom in the American Football League with the Houston Oilers.

My claim to fame is that the picture now hangs on the wall in our condo in Oxford, Mississippi, along with my mounted mallards, pintails, gadwalls, and woodies!

Several years later I unexpectedly ran into Hollis at an Ole Miss football game. It was our last encounter. I thanked him profusely for making me feel famous for a day. That picture was seen far and wide in sports pages throughout the South.

Hollis was a widely admired small-town newspaperman and a proud Ole Miss graduate who worked for The Mississippian during his days at Ole Miss. Sadly, Hollis is now in the Big Grove in the Sky, cheering for his beloved Ole Miss Rebels from on high.

A Rebel and a Vol Face Off

The sky was gray. The air was cold. Snowflakes were spitting through the air; it looked like we were going to find ourselves in a heavy snow. It was November 17, 1962, and the home football game between Ole Miss and the UT Vols wasn't being played in Knoxville. We were in Crump Stadium in Memphis, Tennessee, on the banks of the Big Muddy.

This game was always my favorite game of the year because the Rebels played against the University of Tennessee Volunteers. I had good friends on the opposing team. One of those Vols in the orange jerseys was Larry Richards, a very special friend. We had been guards for the Oak Ridge High School 1958 state and national high school team.

Just as UT sent in a new team on offense, Ole Miss counter moved by putting in a fresh defensive unit. For the first time, I lined up across from my good friend Larry. I don't know who was more excited, him or me. We were busy catching up with each other when I heard a roar in the stadium. UT's fullback in the single wing took advantage of our distraction. He ran past us and almost scored. Thank goodness he didn't.

I got chewed out, and so did Larry. But we both got to go in and finish the game.

The Rebels won 24 -14.

Revenge of the Sisters

I learned a dear lesson when my relationship with Judy hit a bump in the road when we were both home for summer break from Ole Miss. I was in Oak Ridge working for the Oak Ridge Gas Company, digging ditches and missing Judy something awful. She was at home in Flossmoor, Illinois, an upscale suburb of Chicago.

A long-distance call in those days was expensive, so I could sparingly call the girl I loved. Mama and Daddy watched the phone bill carefully. But one night, I needed to hear her sweet voice, so I called.

Judy's sister answered. "Oh, hi, Sam. Judy's not at home. I don't know when she'll be back. She's out with her old boyfriend."

Her sister's words broke my heart. How could Judy do that to me? I was hurt. I was wounded. What could I do? I never thought to call Judy to talk it over. No, I decided I would date other girls when I got back to Ole Miss. I'd show her!

Back at campus to start the school year, football practice was hot and grueling, but I still found time to put my plan into action. I called a girl I barely knew and asked her out. Her answer scared me to death. "I'd love to go out with you," she sighed.

Despite my feelings for Judy, I dated a few more girls, making sure that Judy and her Delta Gamma sisters knew what I was doing.

The Rebel football team had just concluded its twenty days of spring football practice on Saturday, April 14, 1962, with the annual Red and Blue spring football game. As he always did, Head Coach Johnny Vaught called a team meeting for Sunday at 6 p.m. to watch the film of the spring game to critique the performances of the team and the players.

Coach Vaught held team meetings frequently. He was a stickler for details. He demanded promptness for every meeting and practice. He had one simple rule that was emblazoned in each freshman football player's mind at the first meeting of their freshman year at Ole Miss. This rule was never disobeyed because it was so simple and to the point, NEVER MISS OR BE LATE FOR A MEETING OR PRACTICE without Coach Vaught's personal approval. If you broke that rule, you would be homeward bound. The loss of your scholarship was called "Breaking Your Plate" because your days at the fabulous training table were over. So was your scholarship.

Following the Red and Blue game to end spring practice, I had a date with another girl. After returning her to her sorority house following our date, I drove past the Delta Gamma house. My headlights cast a bright beam of light into a car parked in front of the DG house.

Holy crap!

There was Judy sitting next to a guy in the car. He was one of my ΣAE fraternity brothers. What in the hell was he doing dating Judy? Then I saw Judy kinda snuggle up to this guy as my car passed by rather slowly, casting some light on the subject.

I almost wrecked my car. I growled to myself, "Who in the hell does she think she is?"

I drove straight to Miller Hall to call Judy. I wanted to find out what she was doing dating a fraternity brother of mine. The girls didn't have to be in their sorority houses and dorm rooms until midnight on weekends. When I called, it was around 11:45 p.m. One of Judy's roommates answered the phone. When I asked to speak to Judy the roomie said, "Hi Sam, she's not in yet. Would you like for me to have her call you?"

I decided to just call back, which I did every few minutes and got the same message. Damn, I was miserable.

I called again at 12:15 a.m. and got a different DG who answered the phone. I was told that she would have to find Judy because a group of girls were in Judy's room talking about their dates.

I envisioned what she looked like with her cute, pretty face framed in a gorgeous smile, blonde hair bouncing as she laughed and talked with her sorority sisters. She was truly one of the prettiest girls on our campus. But to me, she was the most beautiful girl in the world.

So why in the hell was I dating anyone else? That is the $64,000 question that was on the verge of being answered. I will not dwell on the girls that I dated because I'm going to dwell on the one that I love with all my heart and soul. Judy knew about my exploits and so did her sorority sisters. Of course, she was deeply hurt. She was confused. She was angry. She did not come to the phone.

She was at a loss as to what she should do about her roaming boyfriend. Well, it turns out that the sorority sisters had gotten together and created a well-devised plan for Mr. Sam "Smart Ass" Owen.

I'll never forget the day I finally did get a soon-to-be-famous phone call from Judy. I was in my dorm room at Miller Hall, the athletic dorm that housed the Ole Miss football team.

The telephone rang in the varsity hall where I lived. There were no private phones in the rooms because the coaches didn't want distractions occupying the minds of the players. After all, we were here to play football not to talk all night to girls on the phone. Football players were athletes in training and a phone in the rooms could become a menace after bed check.

I answered the phone in the hall and lo and behold I recognized the voice; it was Judy. She asked, "What are you doing?"

My response was simple, "I'm not doing anything. I'm just waiting for the six o'clock meeting Coach Vaught has called for the football team. Why, what do you want?"

Judy responded, "Let's go for ride. I'll come pick you up and we can drive up to Sardis."

"Okay, but remember, I have to be back before six o'clock, or I'll be in real trouble. You know coach Vaught doesn't tolerate being late for meetings. He'll throw me off the team if I'm late."

Judy told me, "That won't be a problem. I'll get back to campus well before your meeting."

With Judy's assurance that she would be back in time for the meeting I said, "That's good. That'll be a lot of fun. Come get me."

I didn't realize that Judy's sorority sisters had been working on a plan to help Judy get her revenge.

Much too late, I remembered that she said, "I'll be back," not, "*We'll* be back."

This is how it happened. One of Judy's sorority sisters had a brand-new car, a black, Ford, two-door, hardtop coupe. It was a beautiful car with a spare tire encased in a chrome cover on the rear of the car. This sleek car also had a brand-new feature on it: automatic door locks.

Judy was going to take Sam for the ride of his life; he just didn't know it. She arrived in front of Miller Hall in her sorority sister's car. It was 4:15 p.m. As always, she looked adorable sitting behind the steering wheel of that fancy car.

Judy flashed me one of her beautiful smiles, and I began to melt. I trotted to the car, got inside, and said, "Man, this is a beautiful car. Almost as pretty as you. Whose is it?"

Judy smiled and said, "It belongs to one of my sorority sisters. Isn't it pretty?"

I said, "Yeah. I wish I had one like this."

Judy said, "Your car's just as nice, and it's a convertible."

I realized she was right because I owned a 1957 Chevrolet convertible that was light green with a white top and pale green and white, rolled leather interior.

Judy knew where she was going, but her passenger didn't. I thought we were just going to ride around Oxford a little bit or maybe go to the Ole Miss Drive In to get a Coke.

Unbeknownst to me, that wasn't a part of the plan. I was becoming a bit antsy about the time and the mandatory football team meeting that Coach Vaught had called. I was totally oblivious to the fact that Judy was taking me to a predetermined destination accessible only by a dusty, red clay and gravel road in northern Mississippi. Her destination was a landing on the shore of the huge flood control body of water known as Sardis Lake.

Judy had really been concerned about this trip. Not because of her plan and what was about to happen to me, but because the beautiful, black, Ford hardtop she was driving would be covered with red clay dust after the ride.

Her sorority sister who owned the automobile told Judy, "No worries, little sister. It'll be worth washing the car once

Sam has been taught his lesson: 'Don't mess with Our Delta Gamma sisters.'"

Judy turned the borrowed car west back toward the Ole Miss campus and Miller Hall, the football dormitory a short distance away. I felt less apprehensive about being tardy for the team meeting. Then Judy turned down Sorority Row and drove past the Delta Gamma house. All her sorority sisters were in the front yard or on the front porch. They waved at Judy and clapped as she drove by on her way to Sardis Lake.

None of the waves were for me. I was persona non grata!

I said to Judy, "What are you doing? I have to be back before six o'clock. I can't be late for the meeting with Coach Vaught."

Judy assured me, "Quit worrying. All is well. We're just going to drive up to Sardis Lake because I need to talk with you."

The drive to Sardis seemed to take forever for both of us. I didn't know what was going on. Judy looked a little nervous, too.

Making the drive to Sardis a little more difficult than usual was the new coat of gravel that had just been scattered on the road by the Mississippi Highway Department.

A light bulb came on in Judy's head. That new gravel would play an instrumental part to her plan. The gravel was deep and made it difficult to drive, especially for Judy.

Judy was from a beautiful suburb of Chicago, and they didn't have gravel roads in the Windy City. Mississippi was a new experience for her. So were gravel roads, and so was her southern boyfriend. Judy had never been to the South for any length of time except when passing through when she and her family drove to Florida for vacations.

But I had really put a new twist on our relationship when I started dating other girls.

Our summer spat, thanks to Judy's little sister, spun into fall. That turned out to be inaccurate, but I didn't know that. Now here she was in a borrowed car, riding on a dirt and gravel road in Mississippi, worrying about losing her sweetheart.

Meanwhile, her sweetheart was sitting by her side in a borrowed car being navigated by a girl he'd treated like a stray dog. He was more worried about being late to a football meeting with Coach Vaught and losing his scholarship than making her happy.

I turned to Judy and asked, "Where are we going? I have to be at Miller Hall before six o'clock because I ain't gonna lose my scholarship. Why don't you turn around?"

Judy was becoming a bit antsy and replied, "Don't worry, we're going to Sardis and we're almost there. You should be back in time for your meeting."

That comment caught me off guard, but not as much as the next turn of events. Judy decided to execute the plan right then.

She had arrived at the predetermined destination. Judy pulled over to the side of the graveled road and said, "I think I have a flat tire. Would you mind checking for me, Sam?"

With that comment, my heart just about stopped beating. I looked at my Sugar Bowl watch and the time was 5:10 p.m. Coach Vaught's called team meeting was to start in exactly fifty minutes, assuming that my watch's time was correct.

I got out of the car to start checking the tires for a flat. I glanced at my watch. It was now 5:15. I hurriedly checked the tires. Thank God, no flats.

I returned to the door on the passenger side of the car to get in for the ride back to campus.

Right then I heard a horrible sound. It was a sound I had never heard before, an unusual sound, a kinda loud click with a hint of a thud resonating from within the car. I had just been introduced to electric door locks for the first time in my life. I was locked out of the most beautiful car on this gravelly dirt road at least thirty minutes from the Ole Miss campus. Was I locked out on purpose? Or did my sweet Judy simply hit the electric door lock button by mistake?

At exactly 5:31 p.m., Judy motioned me to come to her side of the car. I did as she requested. That's when she cracked her window slightly and gave me the rehearsed speech that she and her Delta Gamma sisters had prepared for me. Her message was clear. Precise. Heartfelt. Powerful. Devastating.

Basically, she told me I had broken her heart and that she never wanted to see me again.

Then she drove away.

As I stood there in the middle of nowhere, I watched the taillights of Judy's borrowed car go over the first hill.

I thought to myself that she would be back because she got her point across. Plus, being the sweet, kind, and loving girl that she is, she wouldn't want me to lose my scholarship for being late for Coach Vaught's meeting.

The tail lights went over the second hill, then the third hill. The last glimpse of the disappearing car sent a horrible chill down my spine and a clear message to me. *She ain't coming back!*

It was a warm day. The humidity was unusually high for the time of year and the late afternoon. I started running toward the Ole Miss Campus. I was dressed in khaki trousers, a blue button-down collar dress shirt, and brand-new Bostonian loafers that were the stylish rage on campus.

But those shoes weren't worth a tinker's damn for running. Especially on a warm spring day on a North Mississippi gravel road and a long way to go with a short time to get there. I was a doomed man.

All of a sudden, I heard the crunch of tires on the gravel. I stopped running and turned to see an approaching pickup truck. It was a dilapidated rattle-trap, black in color, with a thick film of Mississippi red clay dust all over it.

I began flagging the truck down, hoping the driver would stop. Thank God he did. I ran around to the driver's side of the truck and asked the driver if he was headed for town. Thank the Lord he said he was. Then I asked him if I could get a ride to Miller Hall. He thought for a few seconds. "Whuh dat at?"

I told him and he finally said okay.

I started to get in the passenger side of the truck when he held up his hand and told me to get in the back of the truck with his dog, a black and tan coon hound, slobbering and drooling.

I climbed in back of the truck and away we went toward town. I was sweating up a storm because I had been running for a while. I was hot, and my adrenalin was flowing fast. I checked my watch.

Holy shit! It was going to be close. I had lost my girlfriend. I was on the verge of losing my scholarship. And I was at the mercy of an old man with a black and tan coonhound slobbering all over me.

It was 5:58 p.m. when the old pickup pulled up in front of Miller Hall. I jumped out of the back of that truck, threw the driver the only five dollars I had to my name, and sprinted toward the meeting room.

As I ran down the hall full speed, I busted into the meeting as the clock clicked to exactly 6 p.m. Coach Vaught arrived at the podium as I made my entrance. The room exploded into laughter.

There was one empty seat in the center of the room reserved just for me. I was completely covered in sweat and red clay dust, which had now become a red clay mud cake.

Coach Vaught looked at me and said, "Where in the hell have you been?

Then I realized that my teammates had been in on the scheme that the Delta Gammas had planned and orchestrated so well. Little did I know, but Coach Wobble Davidson's wife, Mrs. Sarah Davidson, was a Delta Gamma alumnae. She was the alumni advisor to the Delta Gamma Chapter. She had also been an advisor on the plan.

I learned a lot of lessons that horrible day. But most importantly, I learned that I should communicate with the woman I loved instead of acting like a hurt puppy.

The Lifers: A Band of Convicts

The last Christmas dance I remember was at Ole Miss in 1961. The Christmas Dance at Miller Hall was a rich tradition. The football team always threw a big shindig with music provided by a mystery band.

I didn't have a date. Judy and I had (temporarily) broken up earlier in the year because of bogus information provided by her younger sister. That debacle should never have happened, but it did; it almost ruined a spectacular romance between two true lovers.

Since I didn't have a date, I was free to dance with whomever I pleased. I arrived at the party a bit early, because I wanted to hear the band warming up.

Surprisingly, the instruments and sound equipment were all in place, but there was no band. The dance was to begin at 7 p.m., but that would be impossible without music. Where was the band?

When the clock struck 7 p.m., the partygoers started arriving in droves. A very impressive crowd; beautiful Ole Miss coeds, big, well-dressed, nice-looking athletes, champions in football and baseball. They were obviously ready to party. In fact, most had been partying before they arrived. Johnny's Grocery, our favorite bootlegger, located fifteen miles from Ole Miss, was doing land-office business.

The atmosphere was electric, but was no damn music! Once everyone realized there was no music, they began to wonder if there would be a dance or not. They started looking around, growing antsy. The crowd was about to disperse and go somewhere the brown water was flowing, and then it happened!

A strange sound started emanating throughout Miller Hall.

"Hooh! Aah! Hooh! Aah! Hooh! Aah…"

What in the world was that strange sound?

Entering Miller Hall through the glass front doors was a large group of convicts. They headed straight toward the large dining area that had been converted into a fabulously decorated dance hall. This was the band.

There were at least thirty of them, plus several guards armed with shotguns. The band wore black-and-white striped prison uniforms, with chains on their ankles. They were all colored. Remember, this was 1961. They marched to their designated positions, pausing with each step, still chanting, "Hooh! Aah! Hooh! Aah!"

The chanting stopped when the trustees were situated in their proper positions. The longest, lankiest convict, who appeared to be the band's leader, stepped up to the microphone. In a deep, gravelly voice, he said, "Merry Christmas Y'all! We hopes you has fun tonight. We're the Lifers, from Parchman Farm. Here's our first song. We hopes y'all likes it."

With that, the Lifers broke out singing:
Hooh! Aah! Hooh! Aah!

Uh! Aah! Uh! Aah!
Well don't you know?
That's the sound of the men
Working on the chain ga-a-ang
That's the sound of the men
Working on the chain gang . . .

The partygoers went wild. The Lifers were obviously proud, because they all claimed to be big Ole Miss fans.

The all-white guard contingent was obviously pissed off at the world. One guard asked me, "Why are these nigger convicts having so much fun and we have to watch over them?"

My response was quick: "If you think you're as good as them, go up there and sing with 'em!"

Lo and behold, he did. And he was really good! Even though he was a guard and white, he fit right in. The convicts were surprised and so were we. Holy shit! *Was this a revelation,* I said to myself.

Time flies when you're having fun. Maybe it was a revelation! A white prison guard, singing with a colored band filled with lifer convicts at Miller Hall in Oxford, Mississippi, on the campus of Ole Miss. Amazing! To this day that's the best Christmas party I have ever attended.

Note
"Chain Gang" was written and originally performed by Sam Cooke.

1962: Turmoil on Campus

Integration didn't go well at Ole Miss back in 1962. I know because I was there. After the first night of the riot, I walked out of Miller Hall early in the morning onto a campus that looked like a war zone. I couldn't believe what I was seeing. Burned-out shells of cars were still smoldering around the campus. Puffs of tear gas rose from the grass in The Grove; the smell burned my eyes. I didn't realize that the stench of tear gas would linger for weeks.

The Grove was covered with bricks and debris. I stood there in shock. Who would do this? And why? The riot lasted one night, but the dissension didn't end for a long, long time.

Classes were cancelled for several weeks because tear gas invaded the cooling systems. When school reopened, the campus was still very tense because federal marshals occupied the place.

The material destruction was bad enough. But the human toll was truly senseless. Two people lost their lives. Many more were injured. What a stupid way to protest integration! Why had rabble-rousing outsiders come to our campus? Why did some of our students join the fray?

My high school had integrated peacefully during my freshman year, back in 1954. Here it was seven years later, and Ole Miss, Georgia, Alabama, and other schools in the South were disrupted by riots and political grandstanding.

We couldn't play any of our football games on campus because the 101st Airborne Division was camped in the stadium and on several of our practice fields. Our coaches made certain the football players kept their minds on the games, all of which were played out of town.

Staying focused on the games paid off big-time. The Ole Miss Rebels won every game, cementing a perfect season and winning the Southeastern Conference championship. The frosting on the cake was a win over the Arkansas Razorbacks, the Southwest Conference champion, in the prestigious Sugar Bowl in New Orleans.

Samuel Walton Owen

Inspection with a Bang

All male students at Ole Miss were required to take two years of military science, a.k.a., Reserve Officers Training Corps, ROTC, or ROTCY. Most freshmen football players elected to take Army ROTC because we thought it might be easier than Air Force, Navy, or Marines. Besides, the Army cadre loved having "jocks" as their students. They never missed a game.

Each year the Army ROTC had a major inspection. It was always conducted by the Commanding General of The Third Army, headquartered at Fort McPherson outside of Atlanta.

The day for the inspection arrived and all of us cadets were polishing our brass insignia, spit shining our shoes, and trying to make our instructors look good.

As I was about to leave to report for the inspection formation, three varsity football players who were also high-ranking officers in Advanced Army ROTC came to my room. They ordered me to remove the polished brass insignia from my uniform. Then I was told to remove my shining, spit-polished shoes, and black socks and replace them with the pair of rubber galoshes they handed me.

The big blow came when they made me take off my starched shirt, exposing my bare chest, but had me leave my tie and uniform jacket in place. I looked like a Ringling Brothers Circus clown in my new outfit.

They made me stand at attention for their inspection, which I passed despite their antics. Then they ordered me to join the big deal inspection on the ROTC parade field.

In the meantime, a large crowd of students had gathered to watch the inspection. My varsity friends had skillfully spread the word of what was happening on the parade field.

The ROTC band was playing some of John Philip Sousa's greatest marches as I took my M-1 rifle from its place in the gun rack. I hustled to join the formation waiting to be inspected by the big shot general from Fort McPherson.

When the general stepped in front of me, I came to attention briskly and took the inspection position. That's when I brought my unloaded M-1 rifle to my shoulder into a shooting position and screamed BANG! BANG! BANG! (That's precisely what I had been instructed to do by the varsity players.)

The Commanding General of The Third Army was completely flabbergasted. He yelled at the top of his lungs, "What in the hell are you doing, cadet? Where's your damn shirt? Are those galoshes on your feet without socks?"

My response was quick and did the trick, "Yessir, General. I also shot those three buzzards up there in the sky."

The General hesitated, glanced at the soaring buzzards, and then burst out laughing. The big man was doubled over he was laughing so hard. Then he slapped me on the shoulder and said, "Great shot, cadet. You're going to get the maximum merits for this inspection. I bet you're a jock. I played football for Auburn."

I answered him proudly, "Yessir, I play for The Rebels."

"You're dismissed son. Good job and good luck!"

I took off running to Miller Hall as the gathered crowd cheered and clapped.

The next day Colonel Whitney D. Stuart, the Commandant of Army ROTC, summoned me to his office. He had me tell him the whole story. He was so tickled about the whole situation that I wasn't sure if he would ever quit laughing. But he did quit laughing.

He called the three varsity players into his office. I don't know what happened to them, but I do know they didn't mess with me again. Neither did the three buzzards.

SEC and BYU Claim Oak Ridge Standouts

Several of my teammates from our successful 1958 Oak Ridge High School football team were signed by Southeastern Conference schools. Our team captain, Mike Brady, signed with Brigham Young University

Larry Richards and Jackie Pope, a high school All-American, both signed with the University of Tennessee, while Howard Dunnebach went with another SEC team, the University of Kentucky.

As sometimes happens, a good player can get caught in a time of transition; Howard was a star fullback at Oak Ridge, and later at UK under the gentleman coach of the Kentucky Wildcats, Blanton Collier. When Coach Collier retired and his assistant, Charlie Bradshaw, succeeded him, things changed. Howard found himself playing for a completely different coach; Coach Bradshaw was trying to make his name at the University of Kentucky by emulating the toughness of his mentor, "Bear" Bryant. But he lacked the magic touch of the Bear, who could balance toughness with player development.

Many of the players ended up rescinding their scholarships under Bradshaw's regime, decimating Kentucky's bench. Most teams had forty or more players dressed out for games; Kentucky became known as the Thin Thirty, because so few players were dressed out.

When I entered the game against UK as a linebacker, I was lined up against none other than my high school teammate Howard Dunnebach. I was shocked when he lined up at right guard: "You're a guard now?" I asked. "What the hell happened? You're a fullback."

His response was priceless: "It's better than nothing."

Coach Bradshaw lasted five difficult seasons at Kentucky. Despite the change of coaches, Howard was a winner after all. He graduated from UK to become an early success in the computer business with IBM in research and development. As a computer engineer, my friend spent his career refining systems and developing new equipment and capabilities.

A Different Kind of Pride

Shortly after Judy and I returned home from Germany in 1967, we went to visit Mama at the Pi Kappa Alpha House at Ole Miss. Mama loved being the Pike housemother, and her boys obviously loved her. "Sam, I'm so glad you persuaded me to become a housemother after your daddy died. You made me take this job and I was mad as hell at you. Now, I'm happy as a lark! I would still be wallowing around in my grief if you hadn't taken charge. I love my job. I was made to do this."

Judy and I both laughed and agreed with her. Then Judy asked, "Corinne, have you had any exciting experiences?"

Mama thought for a few seconds and then shared this story.

One Sunday morning about a year and half ago the front doorbell rang around seven-thirty in the morning. I couldn't believe anybody would do that after a wild night of partying at Ole Miss. I went to the door, and there stood this nice-looking negro man in a good-looking outfit.

Remember, it was 1965; things like this just didn't happen, because segregation laws were still in effect in most of the South.

"Can I help you?" I asked. His reply took me by surprise.

"Yes ma'am," he said. "I'm looking for my uncle. I'm told he works here as a cook. His last name is Washington."

"You must be talking about Willie," I told him. "He's my best cook, and he runs the kitchen like he owns it. We couldn't live without Willie."

The stranger asked, "Can I see him? I want to surprise him."

"Why, certainly you can," I said. "You go around back, and I'll meet you there to let you in."

So I went around to the back door. I didn't let on to Willie that he had a mystery visitor. I wanted to watch this reunion to find out who this nice-looking fellow was.

I opened the back door and let him into the kitchen. The minute I did, Willie looked up to see who was entering his domain. It normally didn't work that easily, because Willie was the doorkeeper. When Willie and his visitor saw each other, they started whooping and hollering. They were hugging, laughing, and jabbering at the same time. They were in their own world.

Willie looked at me and said, "Miss Corinne, let me introduce you to my nephew. Charley, this is the best boss in the world, Miss Corinne Owen. Miss Corinne, this is the best nephew in the world, Charley Pride."

Mama didn't really know anything about Charley Pride, because he was still new on the country music scene at the time, and Mama wasn't a country music fan. But she did know what to do in the kitchen.

I said, "It's nice to meet you, Mr. Pride. Now y'all have a seat at the kitchen table, and I'll fix y'all a big breakfast of country ham, fried eggs, grits, biscuits and red-eye gravy. Now, you and Willie just sit down and enjoy being together again."

As the old saying goes, "The way to a man's heart is through his stomach." Charley Pride and Mama became dear friends. Whenever he was nearby during his travels, he always visited her around breakfast time; that assured him a wonderful breakfast whenever he was in Oxford.

A few years later, I was in line ready to board a flight out of Nashville. Directly in front of me in the line was none other than Charley Pride.

Several people approached him wanting his autograph. It became obvious that he was perturbed about the invasion of his privacy, and he was quite rude to them.

After the smoke had cleared, and the announcement that the flight was delayed again, I tapped Mr. Pride on the shoulder.

He abruptly turned to face me. "I ain't signing any fucking autographs."

I was surprised by his reaction, and he was shocked by my retort. "I don't want your fucking autograph. I wanted to ask you a question. Do you know Mama Corinne Owen, the housemother at the Pike House at Ole Miss?"

His entire demeanor changed. He looked stunned for a moment, then embarrassed. He smiled sheepishly. "I do know Mama Corinne," he smiled. "She's one of the coolest people I have ever known. I love her."

"I agree with you," I said. "I love her too. She's my mama."

Charley Pride immediately got down off his high horse. We sat next to each other on our flight, talked a bit, and went our separate ways.

I never saw him again after that flight, because his uncle passed away shortly thereafter.

Fifteen years later, Mama retired from the Pike House and went back to her quaint little home in picturesque Norris, Tennessee. She loved being near the beautiful mountains of East Tennessee. She also became a country music fan, especially a fan of a fellow Mississippian Charley Pride.

Whenever I'm in The Grove at an Ole Miss football game, invariably some not-so-young man or a group of not-so-young men approach me and ask politely, "Excuse us, Mr. Owen, was our Mama Corinne Owen your mother?"

When I answer yes, the response is always the same: "We were Pikes when your mother was our housemother. You're the luckiest man on Earth. We often wish she had been our real-life mother."

The Pike Mystery Girl

After recovering from the initial shock of becoming the Pi Kappa Alpha (Pike) fraternity housemother at Ole Miss, my mama was supremely happy with her new role in life. The Pikes worshiped her, and she loved most of them, most of the time. They lovingly called her Mama Corinne. She viewed them as her new family of over a hundred boys.

Her Pike boys looked after her. They made her life wonderful, and never disrespected her. Mama was the queen bee of the Pikes.

Her spacious, two-bedroom apartment was her nest; her comfortable, stuffed chair was her throne. She ruled her new queendom as she did our home when I was growing up; both places were filled with love, respect, and fun. The rules were few, but followed to a tee.

One of her strictest rules at the Pike house was succinct and cast in stone: girls were forbidden from entering the upstairs living quarters of the frat boys. That was strictly TABOO. There was only one exception: during the open house on Homecoming Weekend during football season, the boys were permitted to display the fraternity house to female friends and family. That's when mamas could be proud of their little angels.

This particular weekend wasn't Homecoming, but it was a huge party weekend because the football team had an open date. Ole Miss was famous for its parties.

The fabulous Piano Red Band from Atlanta was providing the best music in the South. Piano Red's band, also known as Dr. Feelgood and the Interns, was belting out their signature song, "You Got the Right String, Baby, but the Wrong Yo-Yo."

As the party reached a crescendo in the huge party room, Mama Corinne was comfortably sitting in her living room enjoying reading her book and listening to music.

Suddenly, she was startled by strange clicking noises coming from upstairs. She put her book in her lap, removed her glasses, and focused on the peculiar noise. There it was again! It sounded as if someone was moving and meandering around upstairs in high-heeled shoes.

Mama Corinne became upset with her Pike boys. They never violated her rules. Now someone had probably had too much Jack Daniels Green Label and violated the strictest rule of all by sneaking a girl upstairs to do God-knows-what.

Her imagination went wild. Who would do such a thing?

She decided right then and there to go find out. The original steel magnolia was about to make someone rue this day, as well as the day they were born.

She put down her book on the table beside her chair, got up, straightened her pretty outfit, and marched out of her apartment to find the president and the sergeant-at-arms of the fraternity.

Mama Corinne and her boys were going upstairs to deal with the culprit. She was ready to kill somebody; but she didn't yet know exactly who the victim would be.

As she exited her apartment and headed toward the large party room, she decided to take a quick peek at the top of the stairs. Just maybe whoever was up there with a girl might appear and all could be handled without a scene or embarrassment.

As she paused at the foot of the staircase, she was startled. Standing in the doorway of the upstairs living quarters was a strange-looking creature. Mama Corinne had never seen anything like it in her life. It wasn't your normal girl. If it was a girl, she must have come from Mississippi State.

"What in God's name is that strange looking creature?"

It turned out to be a small, black, pot-bellied pig.

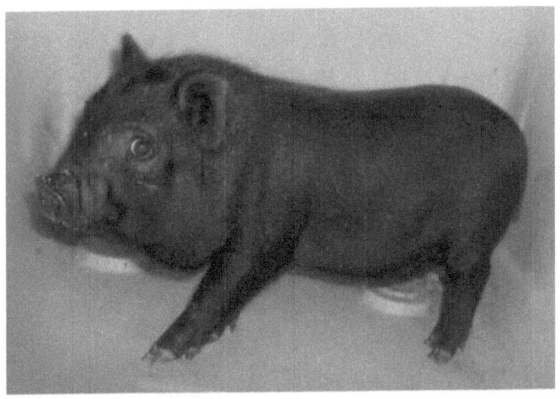

Unbeknownst to Mama Corinne, one of the pledges of the fraternity had violated the second strictest rule: he had brought an unauthorized pet into the house and hid it in his room.

Somehow, the cute little pot-bellied piglet had escaped from its crate and was milling around on the hardwood floors in the upstairs living quarters. Its small feet sounded just like high-heeled shoes clacking on the hardwood floor.

Mama Corinne laughed out loud, and decided she didn't need to cause a ruckus. All she needed to do was ask one of the pledges to find the owner of the piglet and bring him to her apartment immediately.

Once Mama Corinne explained things to the young pig's owner, the mystery of the girl upstairs in the Pike house was solved without incident. All lived happily ever after, especially the frat boy and his piglet; all were saved by Mama Corinne.

To this very day, long after she passed on to her heavenly Pike House, her Pike boys still tell their tales about the Mystery Girl upstairs and their Mama Corinne.

You're welcome, Pikes. I loved sharing my fabulous Mama with you. She was one helluva woman. I share love and memories of her every day of my life.

Mama Corinne Gets the Last Word

Telling the truth is seldom a problem for me, but I will admit to occasionally embellishing it. The one time I knowingly told a lie, my sin came back to bite me many years later.

Let me tell this tale from the beginning. I was living my dream of playing football for the Ole Miss Rebels. I had an adorable girlfriend, Judy, who later became my wife. I drove around campus in the coolest car ever made, a lime-green 1957 Chevrolet convertible with a white top. I was proud of that car. I dug ditches for the Oak Ridge Natural Gas Company all summer and saved every penny so I could buy that used car.

Here's a little more background before I go any further. One of the best decisions I made at Ole Miss was signing up for advanced Army ROTC. The reward at graduation was being commissioned a second lieutenant in the U.S. Army. Another advantage was the annual Military Ball, held off-campus at the Oxford Country Club. We cadets looked handsome in our uniforms, and our dates looked fabulous in their fancy dresses.

Advantage perk was the generous number of libations available at said Military Ball. We took full advantage of the libations, only to be faced with the dilemma of getting our dates back to their residences without an accident.

My sweetheart refused to drive my beautiful car, so, whether I should have or not, I took the wheel. As we were approaching campus, I decided I would drive around The Grove and give Judy a memorable goodnight kiss. As I leaned in for the kiss, I felt a horrible jolt to my car.

The bad news was that I had crashed into one of the heavy posts installed to prevent people like me from driving onto the grass.

I stopped the car, got out and realized that the entire left front fender was caved in. This meant that I could only make right turns, and all the streets to get Judy home were left turns. Was Judy laughing or crying? I couldn't tell.

In the end, I managed to get her back to the sorority house before curfew, taking a roundabout route of all right turns. I arrived back at Miller Hall around the time my teammates got back, all of us in the same degree of inebriation. Our challenge was to get to our rooms before Coach Davidson caught us. Thank goodness, I made it. I hung up my clothes, jumped in my bed, and had nice dreams about Judy.

The next morning, I got a terrible shock. Someone was beating on my door. My roommate let the person in, and did I have a rude awakening! The intruder was immediately in my face, trying to wake me up. I was hung over big-time, so I yelled, "Get your fucking hands off me."

My attitude quickly changed when I heard the intruder's familiar voice. It was my daddy. It seems my parents had decided to make a surprise visit to see me; but the sight of my crumpled Chevy in the parking lot pissed daddy off. He wasn't happy about either my condition or my car's.

"How the hell did you wreck your car?" he demanded.

I scrambled for a story, telling Daddy that I had let Judy drive my car and she had run into one of the posts in The Grove. I don't know if he believed me or not; the alcohol on my breath must have made his eyes burn.

After I told the same story to my mother, she asked if Judy was okay. "Oh, yes," I said. "I took care of her."

And all was forgotten. Or so it seemed.

Fast-forward to some forty years later. My mother was seriously ill and wasn't expected to live; she asked me to bring Judy to her bedside. Mama Corinne took Judy's hand and gave her a big kiss. "Honey, I want to be sure to clarify one thing before I die," she said. "I know you didn't wreck Sam's car. I know he did it. And I'm going to straighten him out for not telling me the truth."

Two Generations of Champions

For a number of years my grandson, Walton Owen, was mesmerized by my 1962 National Championship ring from my playing days at Ole Miss. Walton, an excellent student and all-round good athlete, has just completed seventh grade. His attention is now on playing college football and earning his own ring.

Whenever we're together at football games or other sporting events at Ole Miss or his school in Nashville, I know exactly what his first question will be.

"BoBo, can I wear your National Championship ring?" BoBo is the nickname used by my Nashville grandchildren. My response is always the same. "Sure, you can, Big Boy; just be careful not to lose it! Besides, if you keep on playing like you do now, you'll have one of your own someday."

Lo and behold, when he was in fourth grade, his football team won its first conference championship. The award for that huge accomplishment was the world's largest plastic ring. In his mind, that ring is just as beautiful, important and impressive as mine. I agree completely.

Who knows where Walton will go to college? Or what he will do in life? I've told him he will do well whatever he decides. Of course, I believe he'd have a real edge if he chooses my beloved Ole Miss.

Walton is shown here with my dear friend and writing coach, Sandra Whitten Plant, proudly displaying his championship ring at the Tennessee Sports Hall of Fame banquet.

Great Difference Makers

Great Teachers, Coaches, and Teammates Make a Difference

No one can get to their destination without a map or some other help along the way. This has certainly been true in my case. I've been fortunate to have great difference makers in my life. I'm just glad I was smart enough to let them into my life and let them do their jobs. On the following pages, you will read stories of several of these difference makers.

After graduating from Oak Ridge High School in East Tennessee, I was headed back to the rolling hills of North Mississippi to attend college. I was also taking with me a fabulous high school education.

On graduation day, my favorite high school teacher, Mrs. Nancy Swain, greeted me as I walked off the stage after receiving my diploma. She had taught me two years of Latin and three years of Spanish. She gave me a rare hug and whispered in my ear, "Sam Owen, I'm very proud of you. Good luck at Ole Miss, and always remember, 'A wise man doesn't know the answer to every question, he just knows where to find it.'" Her words of wisdom have remained a guiding light throughout my life.

Two Great Professors

I will always be grateful to the academic advisor to the freshman football players, who was also one of my accounting professors. Dr. Franklin Lowe loved Ole Miss football; he enjoyed teaching us jocks about accounting, other subjects and life in general. He made sure we made our grades through hard work, tutoring sessions, and regular attendance. He was also a very nice man, but he could make our lives miserable if we didn't hold up our end of the bargain. Most of us did well and passed with flying colors. There were a few casualties, but that wasn't Dr. Lowe's fault.

Although my biology class was in a large hall with 200 students, Dr. Irwin Kitchin's lectures were so clear and understandable I felt like I was in a class by myself. He never even looked at his notes. He was the best teacher I ever had.

I did well in his class, although two of my teammates didn't fare so well; on one exam, the two of them could answer only a single question. In our next class meeting, Dr. Kitchin, as usual, reviewed the test. This time his review seemed to take a different twist. "Students, you know I am a stickler about honesty and no cheating," he said. "But I've never objected to study groups reviewing together for tests. It's obvious that Mr. Chester and Mr. Williams spent quite a bit of time studying together on question number thirty-eight. Let me read that question to the class, and I need you to help me. The question was, 'What is the mid-section of the small intestine called?' Class, please give me your answer."

One-hundred ninety-eight of us responded, "The jejunum."

"Now, I'd like to ask Mr. Chester and Mr. Williams to please stand. They had the most unique answer I've ever had on a test."

The two jocks hung their heads and sheepishly answered: "It's the shit pipe."

After the class finished laughing, Dr. Kitchin told the two, "I'm not going to give you an F on the test. Instead, I'm giving you each a D minus for creativity."

Two Great Teammates

After our welcome to the football team, we lowly freshmen were then assigned to varsity football players ("big brothers") as their personal valets. Luckily, I was assigned to two really great big brothers. One, Robert Khayat, would later become the chancellor of Ole Miss. The other was Marvin Terrell, an incredible All-American guard and a great human being. Marvin became a successful businessman and was also blessed with a marvelous tenor voice. He sang at weddings throughout the Magnolia State.

Four Great Coaches

I will never forget seeing Ole Miss head coach John Vaught and assistant coaches Bruiser Kinard and Buster Poole walking my way just after my Oak Ridge Wildcat team beat Chattanooga Central to win the Tennessee state football championship and the high school national championship.

These men were legendary football players and iconic coaches. The knot in my gut was as big as the ball we'd used in the game. Once I had closed my gaping mouth, I understood why so many good football players signed scholarships to play for Ole Miss. I am blessed to have been one of those signees. I also enjoyed a special friendship with most of my coaches.

I've told you several stories about Coach J.W. "Wobble" Davidson. He may be one of the toughest men I've ever known. Coach Davidson was a brilliant chief scout of opponents, and a key contributor to the game plan.

The most important aspect about the football coaches I had at Ole Miss was simple: they were outstanding men with great values who taught us how to play two games extremely well: the game of football and the game of life.

They demanded that we give everything we had on every play of every game, for as long as we were playing the game of football and the game of life.

The great sportswriter Grantland Rice probably said it best when he wrote:

For when the One Great Scorer comes
To mark against your name,
He writes—not that you won or lost,
But how you played the game.

Debits, Credits, and Teal

Another of my favorite professors at Ole Miss was Dr. Eugene Perry. He was a phenomenal teacher, and an even better person. When I knew him, he was Dean of the School of Accountancy, which is now named in his honor.

Dr. Perry's nickname among students was "Perry the Jet." When he lectured to the class, he wrote on the blackboard with his right hand and erased what he had written with his left. That's an amazing talent. I've tried doing it myself, and found it impossible.

I used to go duck hunting every day before class. Dr. Perry's classes started at 9 a.m., Monday through Friday. I normally managed to arrive in time for class after hunting on nearby Sardis Lake.

One day, however, I was late for class. Dr. Perry was not happy at all; after class, he told me to follow him to his office. I was wearing camo and wishing I could hide.

He shut the door behind him and said, "You know, Sambo, I don't put up with anyone drag-assing into my class late. If it happens again, I'll flunk your ass out. Do you understand me? Now, why in the hell were you late today? That's not like you."

I sheepishly replied, "I couldn't get Dixie, my chocolate lab, to quit looking for ducks I had shot. I couldn't leave her. Plus, I had to put her up so I could come to your class." That's when my idea light bulb came on. "Dr. Perry, I've got a deal I want to pitch to you. If you'll let me bring my Dixie to class, I won't be late anymore. She's a chocolate lab, real well-behaved."

Dr. Perry was stunned. His response was typical of the Jet. "Are you shittin' me boy? I ain't teaching no damn dogs. I'm trying to teach you dumb humans the difference between a debit and a credit. Sometimes I think teaching dogs would be a helluva lot easier. Is that your idea of a deal?"

I said, "Yessir."

That's when his idea light bulb came on, as I had anticipated. "Let me tell you what I'll do. I'll let you bring that damn dog to my class if you bring me some teal. I love teal. But if that dog shits or pees on my floor, you clean it up and I flunk your ass out of my course."

I said, "You've got a deal."

From that day forth, the first ducks I shot were green-winged teal and blue-winged teal. My hunting buddies couldn't figure out why I was shooting teal instead of mallards and pintails. Little did they know that I had cut a deal with the Jet.

The moral to this story is pretty cool. I earned a lot of debits; got no credits; and my first delivery to the Jet was eight teal, four green and four blue. I made an "A" in the course.

Oh yeah, Dixie never messed up the floor. In fact, after a few days of perfect behavior, Dr. Perry asked Dixie to sit on the floor near him as he lectured. At semester's end, he gave her a personalized report card with an "A" in accounting. I had to earn mine.

A Salute to Lt. Colonel Whitney D. Stuart

When I entered Ole Miss my freshman year, I didn't even know what ROTC stood for, but I was enrolled in it. After registering for all my classes, I asked a professor what ROTC is. His response was condescending and curt. "Military service," he said. "Reserve Officers Training Corps. Why?"

"I'm in it, and I didn't know what it was."

I soon learned that all male students were required to take ROTC for their first two years at Ole Miss. Since most of my registration had been completed by the athletic department's academic support staff, they selected Army ROTC for me. I learned that I could switch to Air Force if I wanted to, but I liked the Army staff because they loved Ole Miss football players.

That's how I came to know Lt. Colonel Whitney D. Stuart.

Colonel Stuart was a great teacher. He made the military subjects lively and enjoyable. He also demanded that all cadets do the same. I'm glad they followed orders well. ROTC turned out to be one of my favorite learning experiences, especially learning about the battles of World War II.

But Colonel Stuart was more than a great teacher. He became involved with us advanced students as a mentor, advisor, and friend, to the proper degree. He was always Colonel Stuart, and available—until he didn't need or want to be. He kept up with us until he retired, and rode off into the sunset for the last time in his M2 tank. He became close to us, but never too close. He was still our superior officer, but he had some daddy dust sprinkled on him.

As my sophomore year drew quickly to an end, so did my ROTC obligation. While I was cleaning out my desk in the classroom, Colonel Stuart entered the room. "Sam, come with me," he said. "We need to talk. Do you remember the papers you signed a few weeks back?"

"Yessir, I remember. Why?"

Colonel Stuart smiled. "One of those forms was your request to become an Advanced ROTC Cadet.

Congratulations! You were accepted almost immediately, thanks to *my insistence* and your ability. You won't regret it."

I've never regretted my time in advanced ROTC. As added incentive, I would be paid thirty dollars a month for the remainder of my time in ROTC. I was happy about my paycheck.

I was happier still when Colonel Stuart informed me that my request for duty assignment had been approved. I would report to the Officer's Basic Training School for the Medical Service Corps at Fort Sam Houston, Texas. That was a blessing because I had decided that I wanted to be a hospital administrator when I was discharged from the Army.

More evidence that God watches over me. This time it was through my favorite commanding officer, Lt. Colonel Whitney D. Stuart.

A Pope Saves the Day

In high school, I played baseball for the Oak Ridge Wildcats alongside one of my best friends, Jackie Pope. We also played together for the Eagles; a baseball team sponsored by a local civic club of the same name.

Jackie's dad was one of the coaches for the Eagles team; Mr. Reece Pope was one of those difference makers who influenced my life. I'll always be grateful for his support and encouragement.

Mr. Pope had played baseball in the minor leagues. He was a fabulous coach, but a better man.

When we showed up to determine which position each of us would play, head coach Ben Ellis—a difference maker in his own right—told us to take our positions on the field. I went straight to third base, where I normally played. There were two new guys there, but they weren't gonna beat me out.

Each position had at least two players, except for one; there was no catcher. Nobody wanted to be the catcher because it was the toughest position on the team, both physically and mentally. The catcher is the quarterback of a baseball team, if he's any good.

Mr. Pope sauntered up to me and asked, "Sambo, what do you see as you look around this field?"

"Green grass, a high fence for home runs to go over, and a pretty green infield," I said, puzzled. "Why, Mr. Pope?"

In his typical drawl, he asked, "Is that all you see?"

"Yessir, that's it."

Mr. Pope put his arm around my shoulder. "Look again. I see the perfect opportunity for you. There ain't no catcher. and you have a great arm. It's wide-open, and you'll be a great catcher. You're quick, and your arm is exceptional. I'll help you with it."

I looked at home plate; sure enough, there wasn't anyone within ninety feet of it. Nobody wanted to be the catcher, including me.

"Whatcha think?" Mr. Pope asked. "Wanna give it a try? I'll teach you how to be a great one. You're gonna catch the scrimmage game today."

That scared the living daylights out of me.

Mr. Pope had to show me how to put on all the catcher's garb. I didn't know anything about catching, and here I was catching my first game, even if it was a scrimmage. I was terrified. I knew all my buddies were laughing under their breath.

Finally, I was dressed, and we took the field against the other team. I found it hard to maneuver around in all that catcher paraphernalia; mask, chest protector, shin guards, and the fat, puffy glove called a catcher's mitt.

I squatted down to warm up our pitcher. I could barely see the ball, for two reasons: I was unprepared for the sheer speed of the ball, plus the mask was blocking my vision. I wasn't used to this.

The ump yelled, "Play ball. Batter up!"

None of the first nine pitches made it into my catcher's mitt. Two were base hits, and seven flew past the mitt so fast I couldn't see 'em. I was embarrassed. I wanted to quit the team and go dig a hole, crawl in, and pull the dirt in on top of me. Thank goodness my teammates finally got the other side out, in spite of me.

I sprinted to the dugout, looking for a place to hide. When I entered the dugout after that disastrous inning, no one said a word to me. I was humiliated.

Before I could do anything, Mr. Pope came up to me. "Come on with me, Sambo," he said. "We're gonna fix this right now."

My crash course in catching made me feel a whole lot better. Nobody had ever taught me how to be a catcher.

I heard Coach Ellis call my name. "Sambo, you're up. Get in there and bust that ball. We've got a runner on second and two outs. Come on. Do your thing."

I got into the batter's box. The first pitch was a brush-back. That made me mad, and I forgot about my catching fiasco. The second pitch was exactly what I wanted: a not-so-fast fastball. I hit the ball on the sweet spot, a line drive double that hit the left center field fence: Eagles 1, Elks 0.

Top of the second inning. As I squatted down behind the plate, the first batter got a single. It was obvious they thought they could steal bases on me because they knew I wasn't a good catcher.

The baserunner took off and I threw the ball to second. The ump screamed, "You're OUT!"

I turned and added, for the home plate umpire's benefit, "By five feet!"

That was the beginning of a good baseball career.

Remember, I had a Pope on my side. Not the papal one, but my favorite one from Oak Ridge, Tennessee. Mr. Reece Everette Pope, the dad of one of my dearest friends and teammates ever.

Thank You to Great High School Coaches

Sometimes I am asked by friends and acquaintances, "How did you wind up playing football for Ole Miss when you came from Oak Ridge, Tennessee?"

The answer is easy. I played high school football in Oak Ridge for two of the best football coaches ever to coach a game in the United States, certainly in Tennessee: head coach Jack Armstrong and assistant head coach Don Bordinger. They didn't just coach football, they taught us about life and dedication to success. Their practices were grueling. They knew how to coach young men; they prepared me to play for the Ole Miss Rebels. I'll always be grateful.

I was born in New Albany, Mississippi, about thirty-five miles from Ole Miss. The Rebels have always been my favorite team.

My family moved to Oak Ridge in December 1953, when I was in the seventh grade. I thought that move was the end of the world for me: I soon learned that it wasn't. Oak Ridge turned out to be a great place to grow up. Plus, it had always had great football teams, ever since it became a town in 1942, one year after I was born. I was fortunate to have played on the best Oak Ridge High School team of them all, the 1958 state and national championship team.

You Broke My Watch, You SOBs

This story is about Coach Jack Armstrong, my football coach in high school. Coach Armstrong was the All-American Boy, but not of Wheaties fame. Playing football for him was the experience of a lifetime (good and bad), but the good outweighed the bad because we won.

The good times were frequent, because our football teams were always contenders for state and national championships. The bad times were also frequent, because every practice session tested our mettle. Did we have the necessary commitment to survive Coach Armstrong's coaching style? You'd better, or you'd better stay away.

Those who could stick it out were winners in the long run. Those who couldn't last were sitting in the stands at Blankenship Field wishing they were playing under the lights.

Thankfully, I had the mettle to endure. I was on the field every Friday night, loving those bright lights; that characteristic still lives inside of me today. Thanks, Coach!

Tough practices were the price to pay to be an Oak Ridge Wildcat. Our practices were fast-paced and grueling. They weren't the place for the faint of heart. If one was considering playing football for the Wildcats and Coach Armstrong, you had better be sure about that decision. My daddy's firm encouragement made my decision easy. I could face either Coach Armstrong or Daddy; I chose Coach Armstrong.

We were getting ready for a big game with one of Knoxville's better teams. This year, Knoxville East had been having a really good season. They were being touted by Knoxville sports writers as the team that could possibly derail the ORHS juggernaut.

Those words were music to Coach Armstrong's ears. He now had the bulletin-board material he wanted. He was fired up, and our practices proved it. We were getting after it during drills and scrimmages.

It was Wednesday, and the team's mindset didn't suit Coach Armstrong's temperament at all. Little did he realize that he was contributing to the frivolity that was in the air.

He was proudly strutting around during practice showing off his new wristwatch. I'm not sure what kind of watch it was, but it was good-looking and probably expensive.

Typical of Coach's personality, he didn't like some of the antics that occurred after the wristwatch display, antics led mostly by Woody Barwick and yours truly. We had our teammates rolling in laughter and joining in on the fun. Truth be known, we were just relieving some of the pressure that comes with being an undefeated powerhouse in Tennessee and the nation.

Suddenly, though, Coach Armstrong had reached his limit. "Get your asses in the huddle and shut your damn mouths," he yelled.

We knew he meant business, so we had better get straight or face some serious punishment from the master of all punishment. We hustled into our customary choirboy huddle, with the linemen in front and backs and receivers in the rear. I was directly in front of my best friend and collaborator, Woody Barwick.

Coach wasn't through yelling at us yet. His red face made his reddish blonde hair glisten in the afternoon sun. He headed directly toward Woody and me as he cast down his beloved clipboard, sending all his papers flying in the wind; more fuel for the looming firestorm. The loss of his notes enraged him to the point of no return. He stormed straight toward the huddle—and directly at me.

When Coach reached me, he swung his fist at my helmeted head. I ducked; and a startled Woody received Jack Armstrong's best shot to his face mask. Woody, like me, wore a caged face mask; so while the blow did its job, so did the mask. Upon contact with Coach's fist, the face mask rendered his new wristwatch worthless. It shattered into several unusable parts.

Not realizing the severity of the incident, the entire team and innocent bystanders watching practice exploded into gut-wrenching laughter. Coach Armstrong was rolling on the ground, but he wasn't laughing. Coach's hand and wrist were already swelling; they appeared to be broken. He was writhing in pain. "You broke my new wristwatch, you SOBs!" he yelled.

That incident didn't make the evening news, as it undoubtedly would today; parents didn't protest; the ACLU didn't file a lawsuit. It was just part of the game.

This incident became one of those funny stories that make team reunions so much fun. The stories get funnier and better every time we get together. The lore of a football team is priceless.

Perhaps the best part is that we went on to win the game 49 - 0! It was over within the first few minutes of the first quarter, when we racked up 21 points. The final score could have been 100 - 0, if we had wanted it to be. Roll, 'Cats, roll!

Sweaty Palms

Coach Johnny Vaught had a lot of rules, and he expected them to be obeyed. He was extremely strict for the most part, but he did make occasional exceptions. I was hoping he'd make one for me, a newly married man with a wonderful wife and a busted bank account.

He was one of the few coaches in the country who had a rule forbidding players from being married. We were all told during recruitment that getting married would end our time at Ole Miss. "Your scholarship will be pulled, but we'll help you get a scholarship elsewhere as long as it's not in the SEC."

My playing days were over, but I still had a semester of classes to complete to get my degree. Judy and I were married on June 1, 1963. I didn't even consider Coach Vaught's rule when we got married, but I was sure concerned about it as tuition was coming due.

I made an appointment to go see Coach to ask if I could keep my scholarship for the last semester of school. I was quite concerned that I would have to pay, and I didn't have the money. My palms were wringing wet. What if he won't do it?

Coach's secretary, Faye, was always happy to see me. She told me many times that I was her and Coach's favorite.

Faye said, "He won't be long on his call. How's Judy liking married life? She's so adorable. Coach said if all the wives were like her, he'd lift his rule."

The door to Coach's office opened quickly, and there he stood. "Come on in here, Sambo. How's cute thing doing? Boy you got a goodun in Bullet."

He closed his door and asked, "What can I do for you? Sit down."

"Coach Vaught, I have a semester to go to get my degree." With my palms sweating profusely I said, "I was wondering if you would consider letting me keep my scholarship for my last semester even though I'm married?"

"Why are you asking me that? You know I'll do that for you. I'll even go one further. I'll give you a job making $250 a month helping with student ticket sales. Is that it?"

"Yessir!"

"Go see George 'White Rat' Shaddock. He'll fix it up for you. Let me know if you need me. Tell Bullet I said hi."

What a relief! My palms were dry.

Acknowledgments

I want to thank those who are closest to my heart for helping me write my books. Most have never had a pen in hand, but all had encouraging words, advice, and confidence in me. Special thank-yous go out to:

My good friend Billy Humphrey: You have made me a better writer with your skillful edits and teaching.

My dear friend Sandra Whitten Plant, for being my first reader, editor, and encourager.

My fellow writers in the Joy in Learning creative writing group. You make the hard work of writing fun.

My football teammates and coaches with the Oak Ridge Wildcats and the Ole Miss Rebels. You know who you are, whether here on Earth or in the great stadium in the sky.

My Mama and Daddy: One question: does Heavenly Books have my books in stock?

Last but not least. My Judy! You are the reason. I did this with your encouragement.

About the Author

Sam Owen has lived history, and he's made history; and thank goodness he's written about it. His first book, *Old Times Not Forgotten as Told by a Son of the South,* captures the historic decade of his early boyhood in smalltown Mississippi, a time when Sam played outside until dark, only coming in when Mama Corinne called him in for supper or bedtime.

His second book, *Dear Ole Miss*, covers his life at Ole Miss in the early 1960s when Sam lived his dream of playing for the Ole Miss Rebels football team that went to five bowl games, won the three SEC titles and the national title. He met Judy Josephson, the love of his life at Ole Miss, served in advanced Army ROTC, and admired the coaches and professors who prepared him well for success in the Army and for life.

After earning a master's degree in in hospital administration from Washington University in St. Louis, he worked in the healthcare industry as an administrator of hospitals and as a corporate executive for the Hospital Corporation of America. In 1990, Sam and his business partner acquired Cumberland Health Systems, which they sold in 1994.

Now retired, Sam enjoys watching his grandchildren pursue their dreams in a world quite unlike the one he writes about. Several year ago, Sam began writing stories from his life with encouragement from his wife, Judy, and granddaughter, Corinne Owen. Sam says he's not done writing. Watch for his next book, where he shares experiences from his thirty-five-year career in business to help others navigate the workplace.